Historical Stained Glass Windows
Adult Coloring Book

Preston Guymon

Bct. Petrus.

ALWIE DEN HEILIGEN ANTONIUS TOT VOORSPREKER
HEEFT VERKRYGT VAN GOD ALLE SLACH VAN WELDADEN

A·D 1869

Sct. Elisabeth. —

www.ingramcontent.com/pod-product-compliance
Lightning Source LLC
Chambersburg PA
CBHW081119280526
45787CB00007B/2899